The Art of Stress Management: Techniques for a Calmer Life

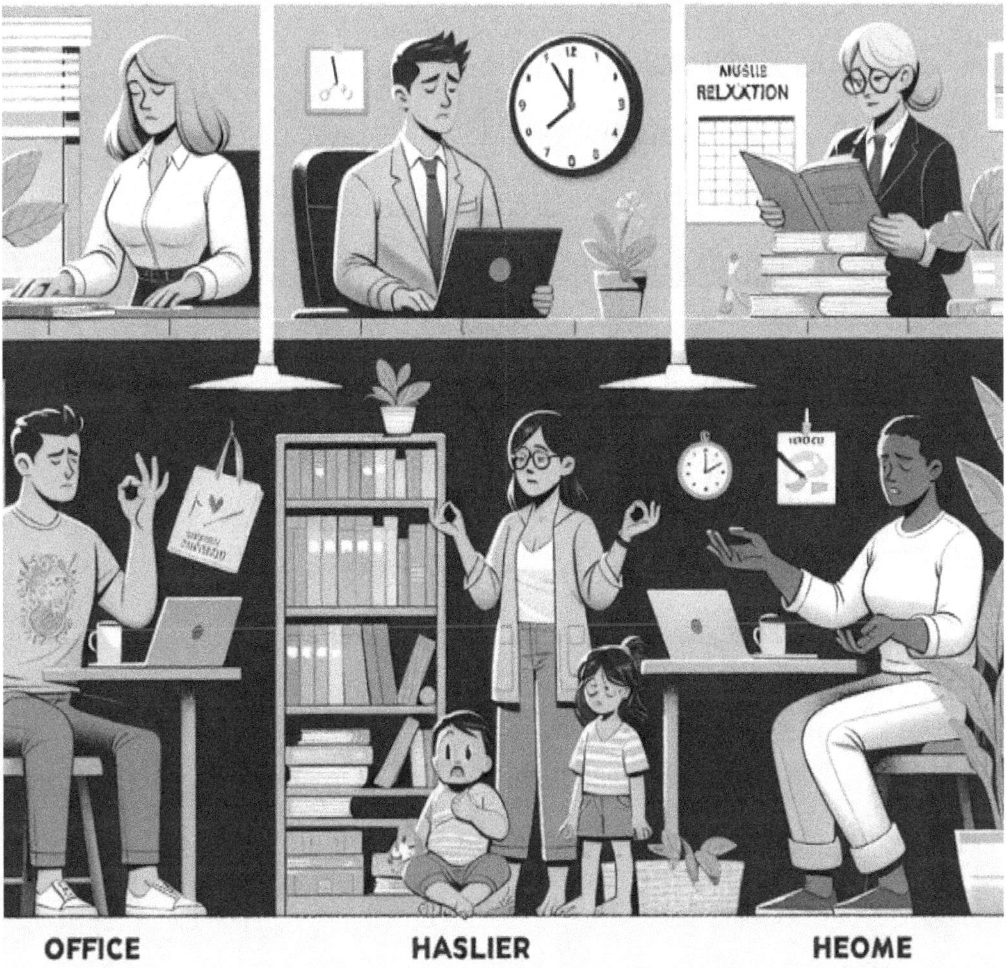

OFFICE   HASLIER   HEOME

Summary

1 Understanding Stress

1.1 Definition and Overview of Stress

Stress, a ubiquitous component of modern life, is typically defined as the body's response to any demand or challenge that disrupts an individual's homeostasis. This response can be triggered by both positive and negative experiences, where the body releases chemicals into the blood, gearing up for what is commonly known as the "fight or flight" reaction. Understanding stress in its entirety involves recognizing its dual nature: eustress, which is positive and beneficial stress that motivates and focuses energy, and distress, which is negative stress that can lead to anxiety and health problems.

The physiological aspect of stress originates from the hypothalamic-pituitary-adrenal (HPA) axis within the brain. When stressed, this system secretes cortisol—a hormone meant to manage bodily functions that are non-essential in a fight or flight situation—as well as adrenaline, which increases heart rate and blood pressure. While these responses are essential for survival in acute scenarios, prolonged exposure to elevated levels of these chemicals can lead to detrimental effects on physical health including cardiovascular diseases, obesity, and immune dysfunction.

Psychologically, stress affects individuals' mental health manifesting symptoms such as irritability, anxiety, depression, and insomnia. The cognitive perception of stress plays a crucial role; how one perceives a situation can significantly influence their level of stress. For instance, viewing challenges as opportunities rather than threats can reduce the stress experienced.

In today's society where work-life balance has become increasingly challenging to maintain amidst constant connectivity and expectations of immediate responsiveness, understanding stress has never been more critical. It impacts not only individuals but also organizations and societies at large—reducing productivity levels in workplaces and increasing healthcare costs due to stress-related ailments.

This overview serves not just to define stress but also highlights its complexity and pervasiveness in modern life. By acknowledging both its harmful effects when unmanaged and potential benefits when harnessed correctly (e.g., through motivating deadlines), we pave the way for more effective personal and organizational strategies in managing daily pressures.

1.2 Physiological Impacts of Stress

The physiological impacts of stress on the human body are profound and multifaceted, influencing various systems that are crucial for maintaining health and balance. When an individual perceives a threat, the body's immediate response is orchestrated by the sympathetic nervous system, which triggers the release of adrenaline and cortisol. These hormones prepare the body to either fight or flee from the perceived danger, a mechanism that has been vital for survival throughout human evolution.

One of the primary effects of these stress hormones is on the cardiovascular system. Adrenaline increases heart rate and elevates blood pressure, pumping more blood to muscles and vital organs. This response is intended to enhance physical performance in acute situations. However, chronic stress can lead to sustained high blood pressure and an increased risk of heart attacks or strokes. The constant state of heightened cardiovascular activity wears down blood vessels, leading to cardiovascular disease over time.

Beyond its impact on heart health, stress also affects metabolic processes. Cortisol plays a significant role in glucose metabolism by increasing blood sugar levels to provide immediate energy for dealing with stressors. While beneficial in short bursts, prolonged exposure to high cortisol levels can disrupt normal metabolic functions, contributing to weight gain, diabetes, and other metabolic syndromes.

The immune system is another critical area impacted by stress. Initially, stress can boost immunity by preparing the body's defenses against infections or injuries during 'fight or flight' scenarios. However, chronic activation of stress responses suppresses immune function due to continuous production of cortisol, making the body more susceptible to infections and slowing down wound healing.

Furthermore, stress influences reproductive health significantly. It can disrupt hormonal balances necessary for reproduction, leading to irregular menstrual cycles in women and decreased sperm production in men. Chronic stress may also exacerbate conditions like polycystic ovary syndrome (PCOS) and erectile dysfunction.

In conclusion, while acute stress responses are essential for survival, persistent exposure to stress without adequate recovery can lead to a plethora of physiological disorders affecting nearly every system within the body. Understanding these impacts is crucial for developing effective strategies to manage stress and mitigate its health consequences.

1.3 Psychological Impacts of Stress

The psychological impacts of stress are as significant as the physiological ones, affecting mental health and cognitive functions in profound ways. When an individual is exposed to prolonged stress, it can lead to a variety of emotional and behavioral disorders, including anxiety, depression, and mood swings. Understanding these impacts is crucial for developing effective coping mechanisms and maintaining mental well-being.

Stress triggers a cascade of chemical reactions in the brain that can alter mood and behavior. The release of cortisol, often referred to as the "stress hormone," plays a pivotal role in this process. While cortisol is essential for managing stress in the short term, its prolonged elevation can disrupt neurotransmitter balance, leading to decreased serotonin and dopamine levels—chemicals vital for feeling happy and calm. This imbalance can manifest as irritability, anxiety, or depression.

Beyond mood alterations, chronic stress also affects cognitive functions such as memory and concentration. The hippocampus—an area of the brain responsible for learning and memory—is particularly vulnerable to sustained high levels of cortisol. This vulnerability can lead to difficulties in forming new memories or retrieving existing ones, impacting academic performance and daily life activities.

Behaviorally, individuals under constant stress may exhibit changes such as withdrawal from social interactions or increased aggression. Stress can also lead people to adopt unhealthy coping mechanisms like smoking, excessive alcohol consumption, or overeating—all of which have further negative effects on physical health.

In addition to these direct effects, stress can exacerbate symptoms of pre-existing mental health conditions such as bipolar disorder or schizophrenia. It is also linked with the development or intensification of phobias and panic attacks. Therefore, managing stress through techniques like mindfulness meditation, regular physical activity, or professional therapy is essential not only for maintaining physical health but also for preserving mental health.

In conclusion, the psychological impacts of stress stretch far beyond temporary discomfort; they can lead to serious long-term consequences if not managed properly. By understanding these effects and implementing effective strategies against them—such as relaxation techniques or seeking professional help—individuals can protect their mental well-being amidst life's inevitable pressures.

2 The Importance of Managing Stress

2.1 Effects on Mental Health

The pervasive impact of stress on mental health cannot be overstated, with its tentacles reaching deep into various aspects of psychological well-being. Chronic stress disrupts the equilibrium of our mental state, leading to significant consequences such as anxiety, depression, and a host of other mental health disorders. Understanding these effects is crucial for developing effective coping mechanisms that can sustain long-term health and productivity.

Firstly, prolonged exposure to stress hormones like cortisol can alter brain function and structure. This hormonal imbalance affects areas such as the amygdala, which is responsible for emotional processing, and the hippocampus, which plays a vital role in memory formation and cognitive function. The enlargement of the amygdala under chronic stress leads to heightened emotional responses and difficulty in managing anxiety. Conversely, the hippocampus may experience atrophy under constant stress exposure, impairing learning processes and memory retrieval.

Moreover, stress has a profound effect on mood regulation by influencing neurotransmitter systems including serotonin and dopamine. These neurotransmitters are critical for feeling good or achieving emotional stability. Disruption in their balance can lead to feelings of sadness, lethargy, and a diminished interest in life activities—hallmarks of depression. Additionally, chronic stress often precipitates sleep disturbances; poor sleep not only exacerbates these conditions but also impedes recovery from mental fatigue, creating a vicious cycle that is hard to break.

Beyond individual symptoms, chronic stress can erode social interactions and personal relationships. It often leads to decreased patience and empathy towards others, increasing conflict and isolation at times when support is most needed. Furthermore, it can contribute to unhealthy coping strategies such as substance abuse or neglect of personal care which further deteriorate one's mental health.

In conclusion, the effects of stress on mental health are extensive and multifaceted affecting emotional stability, cognitive functions, behavior patterns, and overall life satisfaction. Recognizing these impacts is the first step towards managing them effectively through targeted interventions like mindfulness practices or cognitive-behavioral therapy which help retrain thought patterns and response mechanisms towards stressors.

2.2 Effects on Physical Health

The impact of stress on physical health is profound and pervasive, influencing various bodily systems and contributing to a multitude of health issues. Chronic stress triggers a cascade of hormonal responses that can lead to detrimental long-term effects on the body's physiology.

One significant consequence of prolonged stress exposure is its effect on the cardiovascular system. Stress hormones such as adrenaline and cortisol cause an increase in heart rate and blood pressure, preparing the body for a 'fight or flight' response. While beneficial in short bursts, if this state is sustained over time, it can lead to hypertension, increased risk of stroke, and other cardiovascular diseases. Furthermore, chronic stress is linked to behaviors that exacerbate heart health risks, including poor dietary choices, smoking, and lack of physical activity.

Stress also impacts the immune system by altering immune cell functions and increasing inflammation. Under normal circumstances, cortisol helps regulate the immune response by preventing excessive inflammation. However, when cortisol levels are consistently high due to ongoing stress, this regulation fails and leads to chronic inflammation, which is associated with numerous health conditions such as arthritis, diabetes, and cancer. Additionally, elevated cortisol can suppress the effectiveness of the immune system overall making individuals more susceptible to infections.

The gastrointestinal tract is another area significantly affected by stress. The brain-gut connection means that psychological distress can manifest physically as stomachaches, diarrhea or constipation, and even long-term conditions like irritable bowel syndrome (IBS) or gastroesophageal reflux disease (GERD). Stress may alter gut motility and increase gut permeability allowing harmful bacteria to penetrate gut linings thus potentially leading to inflammatory responses throughout the body.

Moreover, chronic stress often leads to sleep disturbances—either insomnia or hypersomnia—which further deteriorates physical health. Poor sleep not only impairs cognitive functions but also affects metabolic processes like glucose regulation which increases diabetes risk.

In conclusion, understanding these diverse effects of stress on physical health underscores the importance of effective stress management strategies. Addressing stress proactively through lifestyle changes such as regular exercise, balanced nutrition, adequate sleep hygiene practices along with mindfulness techniques can mitigate these adverse health outcomes significantly.

2.3 Enhancing Life Quality through Stress Management

Effective stress management is pivotal in enhancing the overall quality of life. By implementing strategies that mitigate the adverse effects of stress, individuals can improve both their physical and mental health, leading to a more fulfilling and productive life.

One primary benefit of managing stress is improved mental health. Chronic stress can lead to psychological disorders such as depression and anxiety. By adopting techniques such as mindfulness, meditation, or cognitive-behavioral approaches, individuals can significantly reduce their stress levels, thereby decreasing the likelihood of developing these conditions. Regular engagement in these practices not only helps in managing immediate stress but also equips individuals with tools to handle future stressors more effectively.

Moreover, effective stress management contributes to better physical health. As discussed in previous sections, prolonged exposure to stress can exacerbate or lead to serious health issues like cardiovascular diseases and diabetes. Engaging in regular physical activity is a proven method to combat stress. Exercise releases endorphins, known as 'feel-good' hormones, which act as natural painkillers and mood elevators. Additionally, physical activity helps regulate sleep patterns which are often disrupted by high-stress levels.

Beyond individual benefits, effective stress management also enhances social interactions and relationships. Stress can cause irritability and impatience, straining personal relationships. By managing stress adequately, individuals are likely to experience improved mood stability and exhibit better emotional responses during interactions with others. This improvement leads to healthier and more supportive relationships which further contribute to overall well-being.

Furthermore, workplace productivity can see significant improvements through effective stress management strategies. High-stress levels often result in decreased concentration, memory lapses, and reduced motivation

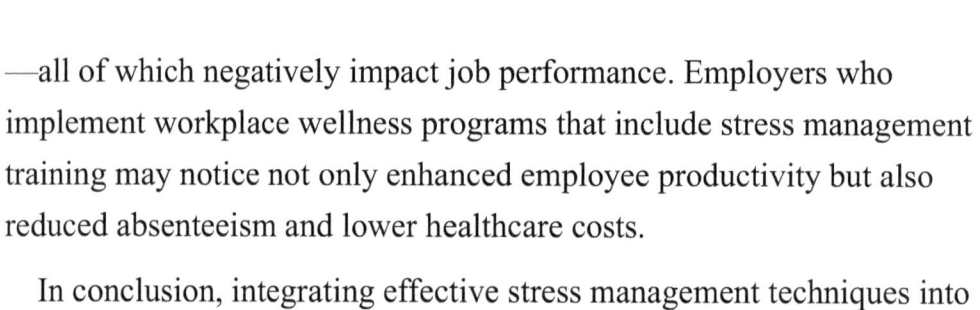

—all of which negatively impact job performance. Employers who implement workplace wellness programs that include stress management training may notice not only enhanced employee productivity but also reduced absenteeism and lower healthcare costs.

In conclusion, integrating effective stress management techniques into daily routines is essential for maintaining a balanced lifestyle that promotes good health across various dimensions—mental, physical, social—and improves overall life quality.

3 Foundations of Stress Management

3.1 Mindfulness Meditation Techniques

Mindfulness meditation has emerged as a powerful tool for managing stress, enhancing concentration, and promoting overall mental well-being. This technique involves the practice of maintaining a moment-by-moment awareness of our thoughts, feelings, bodily sensations, and surrounding environment with openness, curiosity, and acceptance. Here we explore various mindfulness meditation techniques that can be seamlessly integrated into daily life to help mitigate the adverse effects of stress.

The first technique is **focused attention meditation**. This foundational practice encourages practitioners to focus their attention on a single point of reference such as the breath, a mantra, or a specific object. The goal is to train the mind to remain present by repeatedly bringing its focus back whenever it wanders. This method not only helps in reducing stress but also improves one's ability to concentrate.

Another effective technique is **body scan meditation**. This involves mentally scanning one's body from head to toe, observing any discomforts or sensations without judgment. By doing so, individuals learn to become more attuned to their physical condition and release tension held in different parts of the body. It serves as an excellent practice for developing both mindfulness and bodily awareness.

Incorporating these mindfulness techniques into daily routines can significantly alter how one responds to stressors by fostering a greater sense of calm and clarity. Regular practice allows individuals to detach from habitual stressful thoughts and reactions by anchoring them in the present moment—a key strategy in effective stress management.

Walking meditation is another dynamic form of mindfulness that integrates movement with meditative practice. Unlike traditional seated meditation, walking meditation involves focusing on the experience of walking itself—paying close attention to the sensation of your feet touching the ground and the rhythm of your steps.

Loving-kindness meditation (Metta) focuses on cultivating an attitude of love and kindness towards everything, even sources of stress and personal frustrations. Practitioners open their minds to receiving loving-kindness and then send it outwards to others. This form not only alleviates personal stress but also enhances feelings of compassion and empathy towards others.

To conclude, mindfulness meditation offers diverse practices tailored to fit different preferences and lifestyles, making it an accessible option for anyone seeking practical tools for stress reduction. Whether through focused breathing exercises or mindful walking, these techniques provide pathways toward a more balanced and serene life.

3.2 Progressive Muscle Relaxation Methods

Progressive Muscle Relaxation (PMR) is a systematic technique for achieving a deep state of relaxation, focusing primarily on the physical tension in the body. Developed by Dr. Edmund Jacobson in the early 20th century, this method involves sequentially tensing and then relaxing specific muscle groups throughout the body. This practice not only helps reduce physical tension but also calms the mind, making it an effective stress management tool.

The process of PMR typically begins with the muscles in the feet and gradually works up to the face and head. As individuals tense each muscle group, they are encouraged to hold the tension for about five to ten seconds before releasing it abruptly. This release should bring a sensation of relief that leads to greater awareness of bodily sensations and relaxation. The contrast between tension and relaxation aims to increase bodily awareness and helps to highlight areas where stress accumulates.

One key aspect of PMR is its adaptability; it can be modified for different needs and circumstances. For instance, shorter versions can be used in stressful situations to provide immediate relief, while longer sessions can serve as part of a daily routine to manage chronic stress. Additionally, PMR can be combined with other relaxation techniques such as deep breathing or visualization to enhance its effects.

Research has shown that regular practice of PMR can have significant health benefits beyond stress reduction, including lowering blood pressure, reducing chronic pain, improving sleep quality, and alleviating symptoms of anxiety and depression. These benefits make PMR a valuable component of holistic health practices.

In practical applications, PMR is often used in therapeutic settings such as cognitive-behavioral therapy (CBT) for anxiety disorders. Therapists guide clients through the exercises, helping them learn how to relax their muscles effectively during sessions that typically last from 20-30 minutes. Over time, clients are encouraged to practice PMR independently, integrating these techniques into their everyday lives as a proactive measure against stress.

To conclude, Progressive Muscle Relaxation offers a structured approach towards achieving mental calmness by focusing on physical sensations associated with muscle tension and relaxation. Its simplicity and efficacy make it an essential strategy for anyone looking to enhance their overall well-being through stress management.

3.3 Cognitive-Behavioral Approaches

Cognitive-behavioral approaches are pivotal in the realm of stress management, focusing on the interplay between thoughts, emotions, and behaviors. This method is grounded in the principle that negative thought patterns contribute to emotional distress and maladaptive behaviors, which can exacerbate stress levels. By restructuring these thought patterns, individuals can significantly alter their emotional responses and behaviors towards stress.

The cognitive-behavioral process typically begins with identifying specific stressors and understanding how they are perceived by the individual. This perception is crucial as it often dictates the emotional and behavioral response. Therapists guide clients to recognize irrational or harmful thoughts and challenge them systematically. Techniques such as cognitive restructuring or reframing are used to change negative thoughts into more positive, realistic ones.

Behavioral techniques are also integral to this approach. These may include teaching relaxation techniques like deep breathing or progressive muscle relaxation, which help reduce physical symptoms of stress. Additionally, exposure therapy might be employed where individuals confront their stressors in a controlled environment gradually increasing their tolerance and reducing avoidance behaviors.

Another significant aspect of cognitive-behavioral therapy (CBT) for stress management is skill development. Clients learn problem-solving skills to better manage stressful situations proactively rather than reactively. Time management and assertiveness training are also common components that help individuals gain control over their schedules and interactions with others, further reducing perceived stress.

Empirical evidence supports the efficacy of CBT in managing not only general stress but also related conditions such as anxiety and depression. Its structured nature allows for measurable goals and outcomes, making it a preferred choice in both clinical settings and self-help scenarios. Moreover, once learned, these techniques can be applied independently by clients across various stressful situations throughout life.

In conclusion, cognitive-behavioral approaches offer a comprehensive framework for understanding and managing stress by addressing both the mental interpretations and behavioral responses to stressful events. Through targeted interventions designed to alter dysfunctional thinking patterns and promote beneficial behavior changes, individuals can enhance their resilience against stress.

4 Time Management for Reducing Stress

4.1 Prioritizing Tasks Effectively

In the realm of stress management, effectively prioritizing tasks stands out as a critical skill that can significantly alleviate the pressures of daily life. This section delves into the nuances of task prioritization, offering insights into how individuals can enhance their productivity while reducing stress levels.

The process begins with understanding the distinction between urgent and important tasks. Urgent tasks demand immediate attention but are not necessarily crucial for achieving long-term goals, whereas important tasks are those that contribute significantly to personal and professional objectives but may not require immediate action. Employing tools such as the Eisenhower Box can aid in categorizing these tasks effectively, ensuring that efforts are focused on activities that align with one's overarching goals.

Another vital aspect of prioritizing is learning to say no. The ability to decline additional responsibilities or engagements that do not align with one's priorities is essential for managing workload and stress. It involves setting clear boundaries and being mindful of one's limits, which not only preserves energy but also ensures that one remains committed to their most significant tasks.

Utilize technology to streamline task management: Leveraging apps and software designed for task organization can simplify the process of tracking and prioritizing work.

Regular review and adjustment: Priorities can change over time; hence, it is crucial to regularly reassess one's task list and make adjustments as necessary.

Delegate when possible: Delegation is an effective strategy for managing workload. By entrusting tasks to others, one can focus on high-priority items that require personal attention.

To further refine the art of prioritization, it is beneficial to incorporate techniques such as time blocking. This method involves dedicating specific blocks of time to particular tasks or categories of work, thereby minimizing distractions and enhancing focus. Additionally, understanding one's peak productivity periods—times in the day when one is most alert and efficient—can help in scheduling complex or high-priority tasks during these windows.

In conclusion, mastering task prioritization is a dynamic skill that requires continuous practice and refinement. By effectively categorizing tasks, setting appropriate boundaries, utilizing technological aids, and adapting strategies like time blocking, individuals can create a more structured approach to their daily schedules. This not only boosts productivity but also significantly mitigates stress by providing a clearer path through the chaos of everyday demands.

4.2 Avoiding Procrastination

Procrastination is often a significant barrier to effective time management and can exacerbate stress levels. Understanding and overcoming procrastination is crucial for enhancing productivity and reducing the anxiety associated with looming deadlines.

The first step in combating procrastination is recognizing its triggers. Common causes include fear of failure, overwhelming tasks, unclear objectives, and a lack of interest in the task at hand. Identifying these triggers can help individuals develop targeted strategies to counteract them. For instance, breaking a large project into manageable parts can reduce feelings of being overwhelmed, while setting clear, achievable goals can provide direction and motivation.

Another effective technique is the "five-minute rule," which involves committing to work on a task for just five minutes. Often, starting is the hardest part, and once the task has begun, it becomes easier to continue beyond the initial five minutes. This method helps bypass the mental block associated with the commencement of tasks.

Accountability plays a pivotal role in preventing procrastination. Sharing goals with a friend or colleague can significantly increase commitment to task completion. Regular check-ins can provide additional motivation and help keep one on track. Moreover, using digital tools like calendar apps to set reminders or schedule specific times for tasks reinforces structure and accountability.

Creating an environment conducive to focus is also vital. Minimizing distractions such as social media notifications or cluttered workspaces can enhance concentration and efficiency. Establishing a dedicated workspace that signals 'work mode' can psychologically prepare one for productive sessions.

In conclusion, avoiding procrastination involves understanding its psychological roots and implementing practical strategies tailored to individual needs and situations. By recognizing triggers, employing techniques like the five-minute rule, ensuring accountability through social support or digital tools, and optimizing one's environment for focus, individuals can overcome procrastination—transforming it from a barrier into a catalyst for improved productivity and reduced stress.

4.3 Tools and Techniques for Efficient Time Management

Effective time management is essential for reducing stress and enhancing productivity. This section explores various tools and techniques that can help individuals manage their time more efficiently, thereby minimizing the anxiety associated with tight schedules and looming deadlines.

The cornerstone of efficient time management is the use of digital tools such as calendar apps, task managers, and project tracking software. Calendar apps like Google Calendar or Microsoft Outlook allow users to schedule their tasks and appointments, set reminders, and even share their schedules with others to coordinate activities. Task management tools such as Asana, Trello, or Todoist help in organizing tasks into projects, setting priorities, and tracking progress through different stages of completion.

Beyond digital tools, specific techniques can significantly enhance one's ability to manage time effectively. One such technique is time blocking, where individuals allocate specific blocks of time to different tasks or activities. This method not only helps in dedicating focus to tasks but also in minimizing the switching costs associated with moving from one task to another. Another valuable technique is the Pomodoro Technique, which involves working in focused sprints of 25 minutes followed by short breaks. This technique helps maintain high levels of concentration while preventing burnout.

Moreover, prioritization frameworks like the Eisenhower Box can aid in distinguishing between urgent and important tasks. This matrix allows individuals to focus on what truly needs immediate attention while scheduling or delegating other less critical tasks. Additionally, setting SMART (Specific, Measurable, Achievable, Relevant, Time-bound) goals ensures that objectives are clear and attainable within a set timeframe.

Lastly, maintaining a regular review system where one assesses their productivity and re-evaluates their priorities at regular intervals—be it daily or weekly—can provide insights into how effectively they are using their time. This ongoing evaluation helps adjust strategies to improve efficiency continually.

In conclusion, integrating sophisticated digital tools with proven time management techniques offers a robust framework for managing daily activities effectively. By employing these strategies diligently, individuals can create a structured approach to their workload that minimizes stress and enhances overall productivity.

5 Identifying Personal Stress Triggers

5.1 Recognizing External Triggers

Understanding external stress triggers is crucial for developing effective coping mechanisms. These triggers, which originate from our environment, can vary widely and are often intertwined with our daily interactions and activities. Recognizing these triggers is the first step towards managing them effectively, thereby reducing their impact on our mental and physical health.

External stress triggers can be broadly categorized into several types: social, professional, environmental, and situational. Social triggers include interactions with family, friends, or coworkers that might be stressful or demanding. Professional triggers are often related to workload, deadlines, job security, or conflicts at work. Environmental triggers encompass aspects like noise pollution, weather conditions, or inadequate living conditions. Situational triggers might involve unexpected events such as traffic jams, financial pressures, or personal setbacks.

Each of these categories affects individuals differently based on their personal sensitivities and life circumstances. For instance, a busy professional might find workplace demands to be a significant source of stress whereas a parent may be more affected by family dynamics. It's important to note that what acts as a trigger for one person might not necessarily affect another in the same way.

To effectively recognize these external triggers, individuals can maintain a stress diary where they log various instances of stress along with their causes and reactions. Over time, patterns emerge that help in identifying specific external factors triggering stress responses. This proactive approach not only aids in understanding one's unique stressors but also facilitates the development of tailored strategies to manage them.

Incorporating mindfulness techniques such as deep breathing exercises or meditation can also assist in managing reactions to these external triggers in real-time. By becoming more aware of their immediate environment and their responses to it, individuals can mitigate the effects of stress before they escalate into larger issues.

Ultimately, recognizing external stress triggers is about gaining control over one's environment to whatever extent possible. While not all external factors can be changed or avoided, understanding them paves the way for better management strategies and a healthier lifestyle amidst inevitable stresses.

5.2 Understanding Internal Triggers

While external triggers are often easier to identify due to their tangible nature, internal triggers are more subtle yet equally impactful on our stress levels. These triggers originate from within an individual and involve thoughts, feelings, and physiological responses that can precipitate stress without any external provocation. Understanding these internal dynamics is crucial for managing stress effectively and maintaining mental health.

Internal triggers can be broadly categorized into cognitive, emotional, and physical responses. Cognitive triggers involve patterns of thought that lead to stress, such as perfectionism, pessimism, or catastrophic thinking. For instance, someone who constantly anticipates disaster may experience heightened stress levels even in safe situations. Emotional triggers include feelings like fear, anger, or sadness that can escalate quickly and disproportionately in certain scenarios. Physical responses might include symptoms such as increased heart rate or tension headaches that serve as precursors to full-blown stress reactions.

Identifying personal internal triggers requires introspection and self-awareness. Techniques such as journaling or mindfulness meditation can help individuals become more attuned to their thoughts and feelings. By regularly practicing these techniques, one can start to notice patterns or specific conditions under which these internal triggers manifest.

Moreover, understanding the source of these internal responses is essential for developing coping strategies. For example, if one identifies that a fear of failure is a significant trigger, they might work on reframing their perspective towards mistakes and failures as opportunities for learning and growth instead of threats to self-worth.

Another effective approach is cognitive-behavioral therapy (CBT), which helps individuals alter negative thought patterns that cause stress. CBT provides tools for better managing the emotional and physiological responses to those thoughts. Additionally, regular physical activity can improve one's overall emotional resilience and reduce the frequency with which physical discomfort becomes a trigger.

In conclusion, while internal triggers are deeply ingrained and often less apparent than external ones, recognizing and addressing them is possible through deliberate self-exploration and targeted psychological strategies. This not only aids in reducing immediate stress but also contributes to long-term emotional well-being.

5.3 Strategies to Minimize Trigger Impact

Minimizing the impact of internal stress triggers is essential for maintaining psychological resilience and enhancing overall well-being. This section explores practical strategies that individuals can employ to mitigate the effects of these triggers.

Firstly, developing a proactive awareness of one's emotional state plays a crucial role. Regular self-monitoring can alert individuals to the onset of stress responses, enabling timely intervention before full-blown stress manifests. Techniques such as mindfulness meditation not only increase awareness but also help in maintaining an emotional balance by fostering a non-judgmental acceptance of one's thoughts and feelings.

Secondly, establishing a routine for regular physical activity is beneficial. Exercise releases endorphins, chemicals in the brain that act as natural painkillers and mood elevators. Consistent physical activity, whether it's yoga, walking, or more vigorous exercise, helps regulate the body's stress hormones like cortisol and adrenaline, providing a natural method to reduce stress.

Another effective strategy involves structured problem-solving techniques which empower individuals to take control over their stressors rather than feeling overwhelmed by them. This approach includes identifying the problem, brainstorming possible solutions, evaluating these solutions, and then implementing the most viable one. By focusing on what they can control and letting go of what they cannot, individuals can significantly lessen their stress response.

Additionally, building strong social connections is vital. Social support provides emotional comfort and practical help during times of stress. Engaging regularly with friends, family members or support groups can provide validation and encouragement which buffer against negative thoughts and feelings.

Lastly, professional help such as cognitive-behavioral therapy (CBT) should be considered when personal efforts at managing triggers are insufficient. CBT is particularly effective in altering entrenched cognitive distortions and maladaptive behaviors that contribute to chronic stress conditions.

In conclusion, while internal triggers may be complex and deeply ingrained within our psyche, various strategies ranging from self-help techniques to professional therapy can substantially mitigate their impact on our lives. Implementing these strategies requires commitment and consistency but leads to significant improvements in mental health and quality of life.

Developing Personalized Stress Management Pl

6.1 Setting Realistic Goals

In the journey of stress management, setting realistic goals is pivotal as it lays the groundwork for achieving a balanced and fulfilling life. This section delves into the nuances of formulating attainable objectives that not only challenge individuals but also align with their personal capacities and resources. Understanding how to set achievable goals can significantly mitigate feelings of overwhelm and frustration often associated with unattainable aspirations.

Firstly, it is essential to differentiate between long-term and short-term goals. Long-term goals provide a broader vision or end-point, while short-term goals act as stepping stones towards this larger objective. For instance, if the long-term goal is to reduce work-related stress, a short-term goal might be to delegate tasks more effectively or set clearer boundaries at work.

Another critical aspect is the SMART criteria—Specific, Measurable, Achievable, Relevant, and Time-bound. Applying these parameters ensures that each goal set is clear and concise, provides a metric for measuring progress, remains within one's capabilities, holds significance in one's life, and has a defined timeline for achievement. For example, instead of setting a vague goal like "reduce stress," a SMART goal would be "practice 10 minutes of mindfulness meditation five days a week for one month."

Moreover, it's important to regularly review and adjust goals based on current circumstances and progress made. Life's unpredictability may necessitate shifts in our strategies or timelines. Regular check-ins provide an opportunity to reflect on what is working well and what might need changing. This adaptive approach not only keeps your stress management plan relevant but also boosts motivation by celebrating small victories along the way.

Incorporating flexibility within your goal-setting process can greatly enhance resilience against stress. By acknowledging that setbacks are part of the journey and allowing room for adjustment, individuals can maintain momentum without becoming disheartened by minor hiccups.

To sum up, setting realistic goals involves understanding one's limits and strengths, using structured criteria like SMART to formulate objectives, regularly reviewing progress, and maintaining flexibility in plans. By adhering to these principles within personal stress management strategies, individuals can foster greater emotional stability and improve their overall quality of life.

6.2 Creating Actionable Steps for Daily Practice

After establishing realistic goals as outlined in the previous section, the next crucial step in effective stress management is to create actionable steps for daily practice. This involves breaking down broad objectives into specific, manageable tasks that can be incorporated into everyday routines. The focus here is on consistency and practicality, ensuring that each action step directly contributes to achieving the set goals.

To begin with, it's important to identify daily habits that align with your stress management goals. For instance, if a goal is to reduce anxiety through mindfulness, an actionable step could be scheduling a daily 10-minute meditation session every morning. Consistency in these practices not only cultivates discipline but also reinforces the benefits of stress-reducing activities over time.

Another key aspect is to prioritize these actions according to their impact and feasibility. High-impact actions that are easy to implement should be prioritized as they are likely to provide quick wins and motivate further adherence to the stress management plan. For example, preparing for the next day's work every evening can significantly lower morning stress levels.

It's also vital to establish a system for tracking progress. This could involve maintaining a journal or using digital tools like apps that help monitor adherence to planned activities and their effectiveness in managing stress. Regular monitoring not only helps in maintaining accountability but also provides insights into what adjustments might be necessary for enhancing the overall strategy.

Incorporating flexibility within daily practices is equally important. Life's unpredictability means that rigid plans may not always hold up. Being flexible allows for adjustments based on current circumstances without derailing the entire plan. For example, if an unexpected work commitment disrupts your scheduled yoga class, having a backup plan such as a brief home stretching session can keep you on track without adding additional stress.

In conclusion, creating actionable steps involves identifying specific daily actions aligned with broader goals, prioritizing them effectively, tracking progress meticulously, and maintaining flexibility in execution. By integrating these steps into one's daily routine, individuals can build resilience against stress and enhance their overall well-being.

6.3 Monitoring Progress and Making Adjustments

Once actionable steps for stress management are integrated into daily routines, the next critical phase is monitoring progress and making necessary adjustments. This process is vital for ensuring that the strategies implemented are effective and continue to align with personal goals and changing circumstances.

The initial step in monitoring involves establishing clear metrics or indicators of success. These could range from subjective measures such as self-reported levels of stress and well-being, to more objective data such as frequency of stress-related symptoms or adherence to scheduled stress-reduction activities. Utilizing apps or journals to track these indicators can provide tangible evidence of progress and highlight areas needing adjustment.

Regular review sessions play a crucial role in this phase. Setting aside time weekly or monthly to assess what is working or not allows for timely modifications rather than waiting until a strategy fails completely. During these reviews, it's important to ask questions like: Are the current practices sustainable? Have there been unexpected obstacles? What new strategies could be more effective? This reflective practice not only aids in fine-tuning the plan but also reinforces commitment to personal well-being.

Adaptability is key when making adjustments. If certain activities are consistently missed or cause additional stress, they should be reevaluated and replaced if necessary. For instance, if finding time for a 30-minute meditation session is unrealistic, shorter 5-minute breathing exercises spread throughout the day might be more feasible.

In addition to self-assessment, seeking feedback from others can provide external insights into one's progress. Discussions with a therapist, coach, or support group can offer new perspectives and suggestions for enhancing the effectiveness of the stress management plan.

In conclusion, monitoring progress and making adjustments is an ongoing process that requires attention to detail, regular reflection, and flexibility. By effectively managing this phase, individuals can ensure their stress management strategies remain relevant and supportive over time, leading to sustained improvement in overall mental health and quality of life.

7 Healthy Coping Mechanisms

7.1 Establishing Supportive Relationships

In the realm of stress management, establishing supportive relationships is paramount. This section delves into how nurturing these connections can significantly buffer the adverse effects of stress and enhance overall well-being. Supportive relationships, whether they are familial, platonic, or professional, provide emotional comfort and practical assistance that can make challenging times more manageable.

Firstly, understanding the psychological underpinnings of supportive interactions is crucial. Positive social interactions release oxytocin, a hormone that promotes feelings of bonding and reduces cortisol levels, thereby lowering stress. Engaging regularly with empathetic individuals who validate your feelings can reinforce your sense of self-worth and belonging. This emotional support is vital in developing resilience against stress.

Moreover, establishing a network of support isn't merely about having people around; it's about cultivating quality connections that offer mutual benefits. To build such relationships, one must be proactive in communication, expressing needs clearly and listening actively to others. It's also essential to show appreciation for support received as this fosters a reciprocal relationship where all parties feel valued.

Identify and participate in community groups or activities that align with your interests to meet like-minded individuals.

Regularly schedule check-ins with friends and family to maintain strong connections even when physically apart.

Seek professional networks or mentorship opportunities that can provide guidance and support in career-related stressors.

In addition to personal efforts in building these relationships, it's beneficial to recognize when professional help might be needed. Therapists or counselors can facilitate better understanding of interpersonal dynamics and help develop strategies for more effective communication and boundary-setting within one's social circle.

Finally, real-life examples underscore the importance of supportive networks in managing stress effectively. Consider the case study of a corporate executive who overcame burnout through regular engagement with a peer-mentoring group which provided not only emotional but also strategic support in managing work-related pressures.

In conclusion, fostering supportive relationships is a dynamic process that requires ongoing effort and intentionality. By prioritizing these connections, individuals can create a robust support system that enhances their capacity to manage stress more effectively and lead fulfilling lives.

7.2 Engaging in Physical Activity

Physical activity is a cornerstone of effective stress management and overall well-being. Engaging regularly in physical exercise not only improves physical health but also has profound benefits for mental and emotional stability. This section explores the multifaceted benefits of physical activity, emphasizing its role as a healthy coping mechanism.

At its core, physical activity stimulates the release of endorphins, chemicals in the brain that act as natural painkillers and mood elevators. Regular exercise leads to an increase in these endorphins, often referred to as the 'runner's high', which can improve mood and decrease feelings of depression, anxiety, and stress. Moreover, engaging in regular physical activities can enhance self-esteem and cognitive function, providing a sense of accomplishment as fitness goals are met.

Beyond biochemical impacts, physical activity offers substantial social benefits. Group exercises, sports teams, or fitness classes provide opportunities for social interaction that can alleviate feelings of isolation or loneliness. These settings not only foster a sense of community but also encourage the formation of supportive relationships that contribute to improved stress management.

The type of physical activity chosen can vary widely depending on personal preference and capability, making it accessible to virtually everyone. Options range from yoga and pilates for flexibility and mindfulness to more vigorous activities like cycling or running that boost cardiovascular health. The key is consistency and enjoyment in the activities chosen.

To integrate physical activity into daily routines effectively:

Set realistic goals based on current fitness levels and interests.

Incorporate variety to prevent boredom and maintain engagement over time.

Schedule regular times for exercise to establish a routine.

It's important to note that while moderate physical activity is beneficial for most people, those with certain health conditions should consult healthcare providers before starting new exercise programs. Tailoring activities to individual needs ensures safety and maximizes the potential health benefits.

In conclusion, engaging in regular physical activity is an essential strategy for managing stress effectively. It provides numerous psychological benefits that extend beyond mere stress relief, enhancing overall quality of life through improved health and social interactions.

7.3 Choosing Nutritious Foods

The selection of nutritious foods is a pivotal aspect of maintaining both physical and mental health, serving as a fundamental component in the arsenal of healthy coping mechanisms. This section delves into the importance of making informed food choices and how these decisions impact overall well-being.

Eating a balanced diet rich in vitamins, minerals, and other essential nutrients helps fortify the body's defenses against stress and disease. Foods high in antioxidants, such as berries, nuts, and green leafy vegetables, can reduce oxidative stress and inflammation in the body. These elements are crucial for repairing cellular damage and supporting immune function, which can be compromised during periods of stress.

Complex carbohydrates found in whole grains like oats, quinoa, and brown rice are vital for sustained energy levels. They aid in the steady release of glucose into your bloodstream, preventing spikes in blood sugar that can lead to mood swings or fatigue. Incorporating lean proteins such as fish, poultry, legumes, and tofu not only supports muscle repair but also influences neurotransmitter function which is essential for mood regulation.

Healthy fats are another cornerstone of a nutritious diet. Sources like avocados, olive oil, seeds, and fatty fish contain omega-3 fatty acids that have been shown to decrease symptoms of depression and anxiety. These fats contribute to brain health by enhancing cognitive function and neuronal integrity.

Hydration also plays a critical role in choosing nutritious foods. Adequate water intake is necessary for digestion, absorption of nutrients, and elimination of toxins from the body. It also aids cognitive functions and maintains energy levels throughout the day.

To integrate these principles effectively:

Plan meals that include a variety of food groups to ensure a balance of essential nutrients.

Choose whole foods over processed options to minimize intake of added sugars and unhealthy fats.

Monitor portion sizes to maintain a healthy weight without compromising nutritional needs.

In conclusion, selecting nutritious foods is not just about physical health but is deeply intertwined with emotional stability and mental clarity. By making conscious food choices based on nutritional value rather than convenience or immediate gratification, individuals can build resilience against stress while fostering overall health enhancement.

8.1 Dealing with Setbacks

Setbacks are an inevitable part of life, particularly when managing stress in a high-pressure world. Understanding how to effectively navigate these setbacks is crucial for maintaining mental health and enhancing overall well-being. This section explores strategies to handle setbacks constructively, ensuring they become stepping stones rather than stumbling blocks.

The first step in dealing with setbacks is acknowledging their impact without judgment. Recognizing that setbacks can affect one's emotions and stress levels allows individuals to address these feelings directly rather than ignoring or suppressing them. Techniques such as mindfulness and reflective journaling can be instrumental in this process, helping individuals gain clarity about their experiences and the emotions they evoke.

Once a setback is acknowledged, it's important to reassess one's goals and expectations. Often, stress arises not merely from the event itself but from a misalignment between reality and our expectations of it. By setting more realistic goals or adjusting timelines, individuals can reduce unnecessary pressure, allowing for a more balanced approach to problem-solving and daily tasks.

Another key aspect of overcoming setbacks is seeking support. Whether it's professional help through therapy or simply talking to trusted friends or family members, sharing one's struggles can lighten emotional loads and provide new perspectives on challenging situations. Support networks also offer encouragement and remind individuals of their strengths and past successes in overcoming adversity.

Developing resilience is perhaps the most empowering strategy for dealing with setbacks. Resilience involves cultivating a positive mindset, learning from past experiences, and viewing challenges as opportunities for growth. Techniques such as cognitive-behavioral therapy (CBT) can reframe negative thinking patterns that exacerbate stress following setbacks, promoting a more resilient outlook.

In conclusion, while setbacks are unavoidable, their impact on our lives can be managed effectively through acknowledgment, goal reassessment, support systems, and resilience-building practices. By integrating these strategies into daily routines, individuals not only bounce back from setbacks more efficiently but also enhance their capacity to handle future challenges with greater ease and confidence.

8.2 Maintaining Motivation

Maintaining motivation amidst stress is a critical challenge, particularly when facing ongoing pressures that can lead to burnout and reduced productivity. This section delves into effective strategies for sustaining motivation, ensuring that individuals remain engaged and proactive in managing their stress levels.

The foundation of maintaining motivation lies in setting clear, achievable goals. Goals provide direction and a sense of purpose, making it easier to stay focused even during stressful periods. It's important to break larger objectives into smaller, manageable tasks that can be accomplished more easily. This not only provides frequent moments of achievement but also helps maintain momentum and enthusiasm.

Another vital aspect is the cultivation of a positive mindset. Stress often breeds negativity, which can spiral into demotivation. Techniques such as positive affirmations and focusing on past successes can reinforce a sense of competence and control. Additionally, maintaining a gratitude journal where one regularly records things they are thankful for can shift focus from stressors to positive aspects of life.

Physical well-being is also closely tied to motivational levels. Regular physical activity releases endorphins, known as 'feel-good' hormones, which naturally elevate mood and energy levels. Ensuring adequate sleep and proper nutrition are equally important; they fortify mental resilience and prevent fatigue, both of which are crucial for staying motivated under stress.

Social support plays an instrumental role in maintaining motivation. Sharing goals with friends or colleagues can create a system of accountability that encourages persistence. Moreover, receiving encouragement or even constructive feedback can provide new perspectives and enhance problem-solving approaches when challenges arise.

Lastly, it's essential to recognize and celebrate progress towards goals, no matter how small. Acknowledging achievements not only boosts self-esteem but also reinforces the behavior needed to continue making progress despite obstacles posed by stress.

In conclusion, maintaining motivation while managing stress involves a balanced approach encompassing goal setting, cultivating positivity, caring for physical health, leveraging social support, and recognizing achievements. By integrating these strategies into daily routines, individuals can sustain their drive towards personal and professional aspirations even in high-pressure environments.

8.3 Cultivating Self-Compassion

Cultivating self-compassion is a vital strategy in managing stress and enhancing overall emotional resilience. This practice involves treating oneself with the same kindness, concern, and support one would offer a good friend when facing difficult times. By embracing self-compassion, individuals can navigate stressful situations more effectively, reducing the harshness often directed towards oneself during challenging periods.

At the core of self-compassion is the recognition of one's humanity and the understanding that imperfection and failure are part of the human experience. This acknowledgment helps to alleviate feelings of isolation as it places personal shortcomings within a broader, more forgiving perspective. Dr. Kristin Neff, a leading researcher in this field, identifies three key components of self-compassion: self-kindness, common humanity, and mindfulness.

Self-kindness refers to being warm and understanding toward oneself rather than ignoring pain or flagellating oneself with self-criticism. When encountering pain or personal failings, choosing to be kind and gentle to oneself can significantly alter one's emotional landscape. Common humanity involves recognizing that suffering and personal inadequacy are part of the shared human experience – something that we all go through rather than being something that happens to "me" alone. Lastly, mindfulness allows individuals to hold their experience in balanced awareness, neither ignoring nor exaggerating their pain.

To cultivate self-compassion, individuals can engage in several practical exercises such as writing themselves letters from a compassionate perspective or practicing guided meditations focused on compassion. These practices not only soothe distress but also empower individuals by fostering a proactive attitude towards personal suffering.

Moreover, research suggests that self-compassion can lead to increased motivation for personal improvement contrary to common misconceptions that it might foster complacency. Instead of punishing oneself for mistakes which often leads to fear of failure and avoidance behaviors, addressing errors with compassion facilitates engagement in constructive behaviors aimed at growth and learning.

In conclusion, cultivating self-compassion is an empowering approach that enhances emotional well-being by promoting healing and resilience in the face of stress. By integrating practices that foster kindness towards oneself into daily routines, individuals can maintain higher levels of motivation even under pressure while also nurturing their mental health.

9 Case Studies and Real-Life Examples

9.1 Success Stories from Busy Professionals

In the realm of high-pressure careers, managing stress effectively is not just beneficial; it's a necessity for maintaining professional effectiveness and personal well-being. This section delves into the lives of busy professionals who have mastered the art of stress management, transforming their work-life balance and achieving remarkable success in their fields.

The first case study features a corporate lawyer named Sarah, who once struggled with 80-hour work weeks that left her physically drained and emotionally disconnected from her family. By integrating mindfulness meditation into her daily routine, Sarah was able to significantly reduce her stress levels and improve her focus. She set aside fifteen minutes each morning to meditate before starting her day, which she credits for her enhanced productivity and improved relationships at work and home.

Another inspiring example comes from Tom, a technology executive in Silicon Valley. Faced with the constant pressure of innovation and leadership responsibilities, Tom adopted progressive muscle relaxation techniques and regular physical activity as his primary stress management strategies. These practices not only helped him manage anxiety but also boosted his energy levels throughout the day. His commitment to personal health has made him a more effective leader who sets a positive example for his team regarding work-life balance.

Emma, an entrepreneur and single mother, found solace in time management skills to juggle her business responsibilities with parenting duties. By prioritizing tasks efficiently and learning to delegate non-essential functions, Emma successfully expanded her business while being actively involved in her children's lives. Her story is particularly compelling as it highlights how structured planning can alleviate overwhelming feelings associated with balancing multiple roles.

These narratives underscore the importance of personalized stress management plans that cater to individual lifestyles and career demands. Each story not only serves as a testament to overcoming adversity through resilience but also illustrates practical applications of theoretical knowledge discussed earlier in this book.

The success stories shared here reflect broader trends observed among professionals who proactively address their stressors. By adopting scientifically-backed techniques tailored to their specific needs, these individuals not only enhance their own quality of life but also contribute positively to their professional environments.

9.2 Transformations by Overwhelmed Parents

The journey of parenting, inherently demanding and complex, becomes even more challenging when coupled with the pressures of daily life and personal aspirations. This section explores how overwhelmed parents have transformed their approach to managing stress and responsibilities, thereby enhancing their family life and personal well-being.

One compelling narrative is that of Maria, a mother of three young children, who found herself struggling to balance her career as a nurse with her family duties. The tipping point came when she realized her stress was affecting her interactions with her children. Maria decided to implement structured family time into her schedule, ensuring that each day had designated periods for work and play. This not only helped reduce her feelings of guilt but also improved the quality of her relationships with her children.

Similarly, John, a father dealing with the dual demands of a full-time job and single parenthood, adopted a methodical approach to his daily routines. By waking up an hour earlier each morning, John managed to carve out time for meditation and planning his day ahead. This small change significantly reduced his morning rush and anxiety levels throughout the day. Additionally, John's proactive communication with his employer about his situation led to more flexible working arrangements, which further alleviated his stress.

Another transformative example comes from Linda and Bob, a couple who felt constant pressure from juggling their careers with raising two teenagers. They started weekly family meetings to discuss everyone's schedules, concerns, and expectations. These meetings fostered a sense of teamwork and allowed the family to function more cohesively. It also gave each member a voice in the family dynamics, promoting mutual respect and understanding.

These stories highlight that while parenting under stress can seem insurmountable, strategic changes in managing time and responsibilities can lead to significant improvements in both personal well-being and family health. Each case underscores the importance of recognizing one's limits and seeking creative solutions within those boundaries.

The transformations described here not only provide practical strategies for stressed parents but also illustrate broader trends in achieving work-life balance amidst modern-day challenges. By adopting tailored approaches that fit their unique situations, these parents have not only enhanced their own lives but also set positive examples for their children on managing life's pressures effectively.

9.3 Academic Achievements by Stressed Students

The academic performance of students under stress is a complex interplay of various psychological, social, and environmental factors. This section delves into how stress impacts student achievements and explores strategies that have proven effective in helping stressed students excel academically.

Research indicates that stress affects cognitive functions such as memory, concentration, and reasoning. Students experiencing high levels of stress often report difficulties in focusing during lectures and retaining information. However, some students manage to channel their stress into a motivating force that drives them to perform better academically. This phenomenon, known as 'positive stress' or 'eustress,' suggests that not all stress is detrimental if managed correctly.

Case studies highlight several coping mechanisms adopted by students to mitigate the adverse effects of stress on their academic performance. For instance, mindfulness and meditation have emerged as popular methods for managing student stress. A study at a large university showed that students who participated in a structured mindfulness program reported lower levels of stress and anxiety, along with improved grades over the semester.

Another effective strategy is time management. Students who develop strong organizational skills tend to manage academic pressures more efficiently. By prioritizing tasks and setting realistic goals, they can reduce procrastination—a common issue among stressed individuals—which often leads to a cycle of increased anxiety and poor academic outcomes.

Social support also plays a crucial role in how students cope with academic stress. Those with a robust support system from family, friends, or educational institutions often exhibit greater resilience against the pressures of schoolwork. Universities are increasingly recognizing the importance of mental health services on campus to provide counseling and support groups that help students navigate their academic journey amidst challenges.

In conclusion, while stress is an inevitable part of the student experience, its impact on academic achievement varies widely among individuals. The key lies in identifying personal triggers and adopting tailored strategies that convert potentially harmful anxiety into productive energy focused on achieving educational goals.

Long-Term Benefits of Effective Stress Managen

10.1 Improved Emotional Stability

Emotional stability is a crucial aspect of mental health, significantly influenced by how individuals manage stress. Effective stress management not only mitigates immediate feelings of anxiety and overwhelm but also cultivates a sustained sense of inner peace and resilience. This section explores the profound impact that adept stress handling can have on enhancing emotional stability, ultimately leading to a more fulfilling and balanced life.

At its core, emotional stability refers to the ability to maintain equilibrium in one's emotional state, regardless of external circumstances. Individuals who achieve greater emotional stability are often better equipped to handle life's ups and downs without losing their composure. This trait is particularly beneficial in today's fast-paced world, where rapid changes and unpredictable challenges are common. By integrating effective stress management techniques into daily routines, individuals can significantly reduce the amplitude of emotional swings experienced in response to everyday stressors.

Mindfulness meditation, for example, has been shown to be highly effective in promoting emotional stability. Regular practice helps individuals develop an awareness of their present moment experiences without judgment, reducing tendencies toward reactive emotions. Similarly, progressive muscle relaxation can alleviate physical tension associated with stress, thereby promoting a calmer mind and a more stable emotional state.

Moreover, cognitive-behavioral approaches empower individuals to reframe negative thought patterns that often exacerbate stress responses. By learning to identify and alter irrational or harmful thoughts, people can maintain a more balanced perspective in stressful situations—this cognitive restructuring is pivotal in fostering long-term emotional stability.

In addition to these techniques, setting realistic goals and identifying personal triggers play essential roles in managing stress effectively. Understanding what precipitates stress allows for proactive management strategies rather than reactive responses. This proactive approach not only diminishes the intensity of the stress experienced but also enhances one's capacity for maintaining steadiness amidst turmoil.

The journey towards improved emotional stability through effective stress management is both rewarding and transformative. It not only enhances individual well-being but also improves overall life satisfaction by enabling people to engage more fully with their work, relationships, and personal growth endeavors without being overshadowed by overwhelming emotions.

10.2 Enhanced Productivity Levels

Effective stress management is directly linked to enhanced productivity levels in both personal and professional settings. When individuals effectively manage their stress, they unlock a higher capacity for concentration, decision-making, and creativity, all of which are essential components of productivity.

One of the primary ways that stress reduction improves productivity is through better cognitive function. Chronic stress can impair brain functions such as memory and attention span, leading to decreased performance at work or school. By employing techniques such as deep breathing exercises or regular physical activity, individuals can mitigate the physiological impacts of stress, thereby maintaining optimal cognitive functioning.

Moreover, effective stress management fosters a more positive workplace environment. Stress can often lead to conflicts or misunderstandings among colleagues due to heightened emotions or decreased patience. A calm and composed demeanor, cultivated through regular stress management practices, enhances interpersonal skills and helps in maintaining harmonious relationships with coworkers. This not only improves team dynamics but also boosts collective productivity by facilitating smoother collaboration and communication.

In addition to improving mental health and social interactions, managing stress proactively allows individuals to maintain a higher level of energy throughout the day. Stress often leads to fatigue because it depletes the body's physical and emotional resources. Techniques like mindfulness meditation or yoga can help restore these resources by promoting relaxation and improving sleep quality. Better rest results in more energy and alertness during working hours, thus enhancing overall productivity.

Finally, effective stress management equips individuals with the resilience needed to handle challenges efficiently without becoming overwhelmed. This resilience ensures that tasks are completed successfully despite potential setbacks or high-pressure situations that might otherwise hinder progress.

The link between reduced stress levels and increased productivity is clear: by managing one's stress effectively through various techniques and lifestyle changes, an individual not only enhances their own well-being but also contributes positively to their professional output and success.

10.3 Strengthened Interpersonal Relationships

Effective stress management significantly enhances interpersonal relationships, both in personal and professional contexts. By managing stress effectively, individuals can maintain a more stable emotional state, which facilitates better communication and understanding between people.

One of the primary benefits of reduced stress on relationships is improved empathy. Stress often causes individuals to become self-centered and less attuned to the needs and feelings of others. When stress levels are lower, people are generally more patient and attentive, qualities that are crucial for healthy relationships. This heightened empathy not only improves existing relationships but also helps in forming new ones by creating a positive impression and fostering mutual trust.

Moreover, effective stress management helps in conflict resolution. High-stress situations can lead to quick tempers and rash decisions, which can exacerbate conflicts rather than resolve them. With proper stress management techniques such as mindfulness or controlled breathing, individuals can approach conflicts with a calm demeanor, enabling them to think more clearly and communicate more effectively during disagreements. This not only helps in resolving issues more amicably but also prevents the escalation of conflict.

Additionally, stress management contributes to emotional resilience which is pivotal in sustaining long-term relationships. Resilient individuals are better equipped to handle relationship challenges without becoming overwhelmed or reactive. This resilience fosters a supportive environment where all parties feel secure in expressing their thoughts and feelings without fear of judgment or retaliation.

Finally, shared stress reduction activities can also serve as bonding experiences that strengthen relationships. Activities like yoga classes, meditation sessions, or even regular walks provide opportunities for spending quality time together while also managing individual stress levels. These shared experiences not only improve individual well-being but also enhance the collective emotional health of the relationship.

In conclusion, effective management of personal stress plays a critical role in strengthening interpersonal relationships by fostering empathy, aiding conflict resolution, building emotional resilience, and providing shared experiences that bring people closer together.

Advanced Techniques and Continuing Educat

11.1 Exploring Advanced Meditation Practices

In the realm of stress management, advanced meditation practices stand out as potent tools for deepening relaxation and enhancing mental clarity. These techniques go beyond basic mindfulness to include methods that can profoundly alter one's state of consciousness and promote significant psychological and physiological benefits.

One such practice is Transcendental Meditation (TM), which involves the silent repetition of a mantra to settle the mind into a state of profound rest and relaxation. Unlike more passive forms of meditation, TM allows individuals to access deeper levels of consciousness, potentially leading to enhanced creativity and problem-solving capabilities. Studies have shown that regular TM practice can reduce symptoms of anxiety and depression, making it a valuable addition to stress management strategies.

Another advanced technique is the Vipassana or Insight Meditation, which focuses on deep interconnection between mind and body through contemplative mindfulness and breathing exercises. Practitioners of Vipassana work towards seeing things as they really are by developing insight into the true nature of reality. This form of meditation is known for its ability to foster personal transformation by helping individuals understand and dissolve their mental impurities.

Zen meditation, or Zazen, emphasizes sitting in precise postures and focusing on breath while observing the thoughts that arise without attachment or judgment. This practice is central in Zen Buddhism, promoting a state of alertness and presence that can translate into daily life as increased focus and tranquility.

Kundalini Yoga, often referred to as the yoga of awareness, combines specific sets of exercises (or kriyas), dynamic breathing techniques, chanting, meditation, and mantras. By awakening energy centers or chakras in the body, Kundalini Yoga aims at elevating consciousness while providing physical and emotional benefits akin to those found in more traditional forms of meditation.

Integrating these advanced practices into daily routines requires guidance from experienced practitioners but promises substantial rewards in terms of stress reduction and overall well-being. Each method offers unique benefits that cater to different needs and preferences, contributing significantly to life's quality by managing stress effectively through heightened self-awareness and inner peace.

Transcendental Meditation for accessing deeper states of mind

Vipassana for insightful reflection on mental processes

Zen practices for enhancing present-moment awareness

Kundalini Yoga for activating energy centers within the body

The exploration into these advanced meditation practices not only enriches one's understanding but also equips individuals with powerful tools to combat stress in today's fast-paced world. As each person's journey with meditation is unique, these practices offer diverse pathways toward achieving personal growth and resilience against daily pressures.

11.2 Participating in Professional Workshops

Engaging in professional workshops is a dynamic way to enhance one's skills and knowledge within their field. These interactive sessions provide a platform for learning new techniques, networking with peers, and gaining insights from experienced professionals. Unlike traditional seminars or lectures, workshops are designed to be participatory, often involving group activities, hands-on practice, and real-time feedback.

One of the primary benefits of participating in professional workshops is the opportunity to acquire practical skills that can be immediately applied in the workplace. For instance, a workshop on project management may involve participants drafting project plans or practicing negotiation techniques in role-play scenarios. This active involvement helps solidify learning and improves retention rates compared to passive learning methods.

Networking is another significant advantage of attending workshops. These events gather like-minded professionals who share similar interests and challenges. Building connections during these sessions can lead to collaborative opportunities, mentorship relationships, and even job offers. Furthermore, interacting with peers from diverse backgrounds provides a broader perspective on industry trends and best practices.

In addition to skill development and networking, professional workshops often incorporate the latest industry advancements and technologies. This is particularly valuable in rapidly evolving fields such as digital marketing or software development. Participants can learn about cutting-edge tools and methodologies that may not yet be widely adopted or understood in their current roles.

To maximize the benefits of attending professional workshops, participants should actively engage with the content and presenters. Asking questions, participating in discussions, and applying lessons learned during interactive sessions can greatly enhance the experience. Post-workshop, it's beneficial to review notes and reflect on how new knowledge can be integrated into one's work environment.

Ultimately, regular participation in professional workshops not only boosts individual competency but also contributes to continuous professional development. By staying updated with industry changes and expanding their skill set through these interactive sessions, professionals can maintain relevance in their field while advancing their careers.

11.3 Continuous Learning and Adaptation

Continuous learning and adaptation are essential for professionals to remain competitive and effective in their fields. This concept extends beyond the acquisition of new skills; it involves a proactive approach to career development, embracing change, and leveraging new technologies and methodologies as they emerge.

The importance of continuous learning in today's fast-paced work environment cannot be overstated. Industries evolve rapidly due to technological advancements, regulatory changes, and shifting market dynamics. Professionals who commit to a regimen of continuous education can adapt more swiftly and effectively to these changes, ensuring their skills remain relevant and cutting-edge.

Adaptation is equally crucial. It refers not only to acquiring knowledge but also to applying it contextually within one's professional environment. This might involve adopting new software tools in tech industries or understanding global market influences in finance. Successful adaptation requires an openness to change and a willingness to experiment with novel approaches in problem-solving.

One practical method for fostering continuous learning is through digital platforms that offer courses from global institutions. These platforms make it easier than ever for professionals to access top-tier educational resources on demand. Moreover, many organizations now encourage participation in online forums and communities where professionals can exchange ideas, solve problems collaboratively, and gain insights from peers worldwide.

Incorporating feedback mechanisms is another effective strategy for continuous learning. Regular performance reviews, peer assessments, and customer feedback can provide valuable insights into areas requiring improvement or update. This feedback serves as a direct input into the learning process, helping individuals focus their educational efforts more effectively.

To truly benefit from continuous learning and adaptation strategies, professionals should set specific goals for their personal development plans. These goals could range from mastering new technologies within a certain timeframe to achieving certifications in specialized areas. By setting clear objectives, professionals can measure their progress and adjust their learning paths as necessary.

In conclusion, the commitment to continuous learning and adaptation not only enhances individual capabilities but also contributes significantly to organizational success. As industries continue to evolve at an unprecedented rate, the ability to learn continuously and adapt swiftly becomes indispensable for maintaining professional relevance and advancing one's career.

Empowering Yourself to Manage Life's Challer

12.1 Embracing Challenges as Opportunities

In the realm of personal and professional growth, challenges are often viewed through a lens of adversity. However, reorienting our perspective to see these challenges as opportunities can significantly alter our approach to handling stress and enhancing life quality. This section explores how embracing challenges not only fosters resilience but also propels us towards achieving greater success and fulfillment.

Understanding that each challenge carries a potential for growth is crucial. When faced with difficulties, instead of succumbing to overwhelm, we can ask ourselves what lessons the situation offers. This shift in mindset transforms our emotional response, enabling us to tackle problems with a more constructive and proactive attitude. For instance, a demanding project at work is not just a source of stress but also an opportunity to develop better time management skills and perhaps discover more efficient problem-solving strategies.

Moreover, viewing challenges as opportunities encourages innovation and creativity. It necessitates thinking outside the box and may lead to breakthroughs that wouldn't have occurred under normal circumstances. For example, many businesses during the COVID-19 pandemic had to rethink their operational models. This led to accelerated digital transformation and new ways of engaging with customers that provided long-term benefits beyond the immediate crisis management.

Embracing challenges also builds psychological resilience by reinforcing our capability to cope with future stressors. Each challenge we overcome serves as a reminder of our competence, which enhances our self-confidence and equips us with the courage to face new hurdles. Additionally, this resilience contributes positively to mental health by reducing feelings of helplessness and anxiety associated with unexpected difficulties.

To effectively embrace challenges as opportunities, it is essential to cultivate a supportive environment that encourages taking risks without fear of failure. This involves fostering open communication in personal relationships or team settings where individuals feel valued for their contributions regardless of outcomes. Such an environment not only alleviates the pressure associated with challenges but also enriches the collective resource pool through shared knowledge and experiences.

In conclusion, transforming our perception of challenges from barriers into stepping stones requires practice and patience but ultimately leads to profound personal growth and empowerment. By adopting this approach, we enhance our ability not only to manage stress but also to thrive in various aspects of life—turning potential obstacles into engines for development.

12.2 Building Resilience for Future Stresses

Building resilience is essential for effectively managing and overcoming the stresses that life inevitably brings. This section delves into strategies that fortify mental and emotional resilience, equipping individuals with the tools to handle future challenges more effectively.

Resilience can be understood as the capacity to recover quickly from difficulties, a kind of mental reservoir of strength that helps us navigate through stress, adversity, and uncertainty with more ease. Developing this quality involves several key components, each contributing to a robust psychological framework that withstands pressure while maintaining personal well-being.

Firstly, fostering a positive outlook is crucial in building resilience. It involves maintaining a hopeful attitude despite setbacks and viewing obstacles as manageable rather than insurmountable. This mindset encourages persistence and opens up creative thinking for problem-solving. Techniques such as mindfulness meditation or cognitive-behavioral strategies can help cultivate this positivity by retraining our focus on constructive thoughts and disengaging from negative patterns.

Secondly, strengthening social connections plays an integral role in resilience. Relationships provide emotional support, practical help, and a sense of belonging—all vital during tough times. Investing time in building strong bonds with family, friends, colleagues, or support groups creates a safety net that can catch us when we fall. These connections not only offer comfort but also advice and encouragement to persevere.

Thirdly, embracing change is another significant aspect of resilience. Change is constant and often beyond our control; however, adapting to new circumstances is within our ability. Resilient individuals recognize change as an inevitable part of life and learn how to adjust their goals and actions accordingly. This adaptability can be enhanced through experiences that push us out of our comfort zones—whether through travel, learning new skills, or simply altering daily routines.

Lastly, self-care is foundational in maintaining any long-term resilience strategy. Physical health impacts psychological health; therefore regular exercise, adequate sleep, proper nutrition are all critical elements. Additionally, setting aside time for relaxation and hobbies helps recharge our mental batteries.

In conclusion, building resilience involves developing a proactive relationship with stressors before they arise. By cultivating positivity, strengthening social networks, embracing change adaptively, and prioritizing self-care—individuals prepare themselves not just to survive future stresses but to thrive amidst them.

12.3 Enhancing Overall Satisfaction in Life

Enhancing overall satisfaction in life is a multifaceted endeavor that extends beyond mere momentary happiness to encompass a deeper, more sustained sense of fulfillment and contentment. This section explores practical strategies to elevate one's quality of life across various dimensions.

The first step towards enhancing life satisfaction involves setting meaningful goals. Goals provide direction and a sense of purpose, serving as benchmarks for personal achievement. Importantly, these objectives should be SMART: Specific, Measurable, Achievable, Relevant, and Time-bound. Aligning daily actions with these goals contributes to a coherent sense of progress and accomplishment.

Secondly, cultivating gratitude plays a crucial role in enhancing life satisfaction. Regularly acknowledging and appreciating the good aspects of one's life can shift focus from what is lacking to what is abundant. This shift not only enhances mood but also fosters resilience against negative experiences. Techniques such as maintaining a gratitude journal or meditating on thankful thoughts can institutionalize this practice.

Another significant aspect is the development of personal relationships. Strong connections with family, friends, and colleagues contribute significantly to emotional support and personal growth. These relationships enrich our lives, providing comfort during times of stress and celebration during moments of joy. Investing time and energy in nurturing these bonds can greatly enhance overall life satisfaction.

Furthermore, engaging in activities that align with one's passions and interests brings joy and excitement to everyday life. Whether it's pursuing a hobby, learning a new skill, or participating in community service, such activities provide a sense of accomplishment and identity.

Last but not least, maintaining physical health is foundational to achieving higher levels of life satisfaction. Regular physical activity, adequate sleep, and balanced nutrition are all critical components that influence mental health and overall well-being.

In conclusion, enhancing overall satisfaction in life requires an integrated approach that includes goal setting, practicing gratitude, investing in relationships, pursuing passions, and maintaining physical health. By focusing on these areas collectively rather than individually we pave the way for a richer more fulfilling experience.

"The Art of Stress Management: Techniques for a Calmer Life" addresses the pervasive issue of stress in modern society and offers practical solutions to manage it effectively. The book is particularly relevant given that a significant portion of the population reports stress impacting their physical and mental health. It targets a diverse audience including professionals, parents, students, and anyone facing daily stressors, providing them with tools to improve their well-being.

The content is structured into several key sections, starting with an exploration of what stress is, its causes, and its effects on both body and mind. This foundational knowledge helps readers understand why managing stress is essential for maintaining mental health and enhancing life quality. The book then introduces various stress management techniques such as mindfulness meditation, progressive muscle relaxation, time management skills, and cognitive-behavioral approaches. Each technique is explained in detail with step-by-step guidance on how to incorporate these practices into daily routines.

Subsequent chapters focus on creating personalized stress management plans which include setting realistic goals, identifying personal triggers, and adopting healthy coping mechanisms. The guide also discusses common obstacles to maintaining a stress-free lifestyle and strategies to overcome them using perseverance and self-compassion. Throughout the book, real-life examples and case studies illustrate successful implementation of these strategies across different backgrounds.

Overall, the book emphasizes that effective stress management enhances one's ability to handle life's challenges with greater efficiency and grace. By applying the outlined techniques, readers can achieve improvements in emotional stability, productivity levels, interpersonal relationships, and overall life satisfaction.